THE WORLD OF ROBOTS

ROBOTS AT YOUR SERVICE
FROM THE FACTORY TO YOUR HOME

BY KATHRYN CLAY

Consultant:
Barbara J. Fox
Professor Emerita
North Carolina State University

CAPSTONE PRESS
a capstone imprint

Blazers Books are published by Capstone Press,
1710 Roe Crest Drive, North Mankato, Minnesota 56003
www.capstonepub.com

Library of Congress Cataloging-in-Publication Data
Clay, Kathryn.
Robots at your service : from the factory to your home / by Kathryn Clay.
pages cm.—(Blazers. The world of robots)
Includes bibliographical references and index.
Audience: Ages 8-10.
Summary: "Describes a variety of robots used by businesses, hospitals, and
individuals"—Provided by publisher.
ISBN 978-1-4765-3973-7 (library binding)
ISBN 978-1-4765-5113-5 (paperback)
ISBN 978-1-4765-5954-4 (ebook pdf)
1. Robots—Juvenile literature. I. Title.
TJ211.2.C54 2014
629.8'92—dc23   2013028205

Editorial Credits
Aaron Sautter, editor; Ted Williams, designer; Eric Gohl, media researcher;
Eric Manske, production specialist

Photo Credits
BigStockPhoto.com: ArtOfPhoto, 13; iStockphotos: ricardoazoury, 7, Torsten
Stahlberg, cover (bottom right); Getty Images: Ulrich Baumgarten, 19; Newscom:
AFLO/Natsuki Sakai, 22, Getty Images/AFP/STR, 28, KRT/Lew Stamp, 4, Kyodo
News, 14, Shamukov Ruslan Itar-Tass Photos, 27, ZUMA Press/Kevin Sullivan,
25, ZUMA Press/Xinhua, 17; Science Source: Ed Young, 8; Shutterstock: Ivan
Nikulin, cover (top); SuperStock: Prisma, cover (bottom left); University of Illinois
at Urbana-Champaign: Department of Agricultural & Biological Engineering, 21;
Wikipedia: 10, 11

Printed in the United States of America in Stevens Point, Wisconsin.
092013   007768WZS14

TABLE OF CONTENTS

Robot lawn mowers help
make yardwork easier.

At Your Service

Robots can look like insects, dogs, or even humans. But whatever their shape, robots are made to help people. No matter where you are, a robot helper is probably nearby.

robot—a machine programmed to do jobs usually performed by a person

FACTORY BUILDERS

TIRELESS WORKERS

Robots started working in factories in the 1960s. Robots don't get bored or tired. They are perfect for jobs that are too dirty, dull, or dangerous for people.

ROBOT FACT
The first factory robotic arm was called Unimate. The big, strong arm stacked hot metal plates in a car factory.

Robotic arms often do difficult and dangerous jobs in car factories.

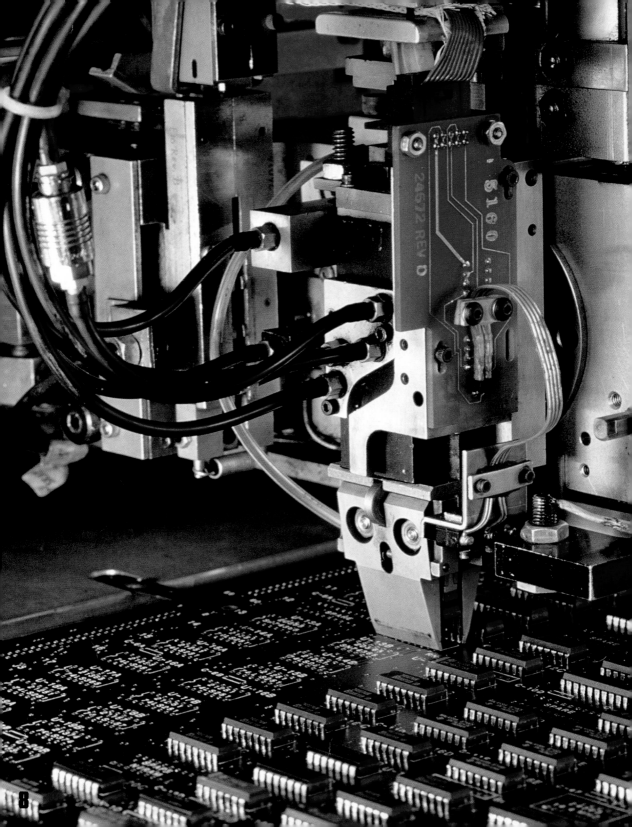

ROBOTIC ARMS

Robotic arms help build products like cars and electronics. Small robot "fingers" handle **microchips** and other tiny parts.

microchip—a tiny circuit that processes information in a computer

AUTOMATIC GUIDED VEHICLES (AGVS)

Some warehouses use robotic forklifts. These strong robots carry heavy loads and place them onto trucks. AGVs sense and follow wires placed in the warehouse floor.

ROBOT FACT

A shipping port in the Netherlands uses more than 100 robotic AGVs. These powerful rolling robots help load and unload ships.

Everyday Helpers

HELPFUL HOUSE CLEANERS

Tired of doing housework? Roomba vacuums and Scooba mops help clean floors. These robots use **sensors** to avoid obstacles like furniture and stairs.

sensor—an instrument that detects changes and sends information to a controlling device

ROBOT FACT
More than 7 million Roombas currently clean floors in homes around the world.

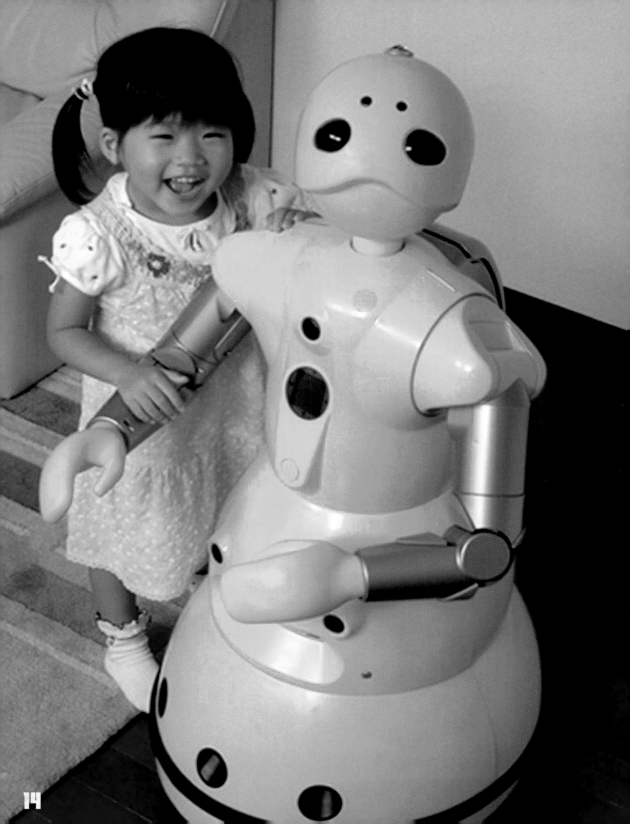

WAKAMARU

Wakamaru is a small, yellow **humanoid** robot. It helps people in their homes. The robot reminds people about appointments or when to take medicine. It can also call for help in an emergency.

humanoid—having human form or characteristics

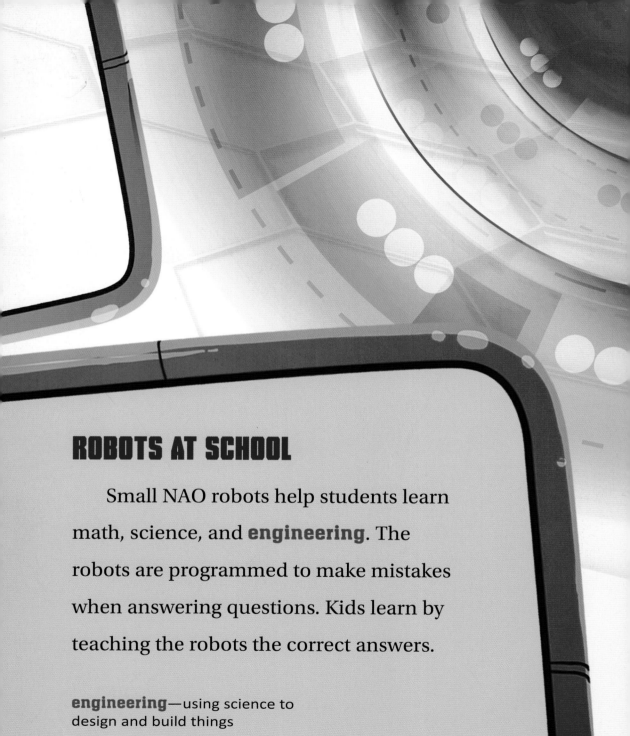

ROBOTS AT SCHOOL

Small NAO robots help students learn math, science, and **engineering**. The robots are programmed to make mistakes when answering questions. Kids learn by teaching the robots the correct answers.

engineering—using science to design and build things

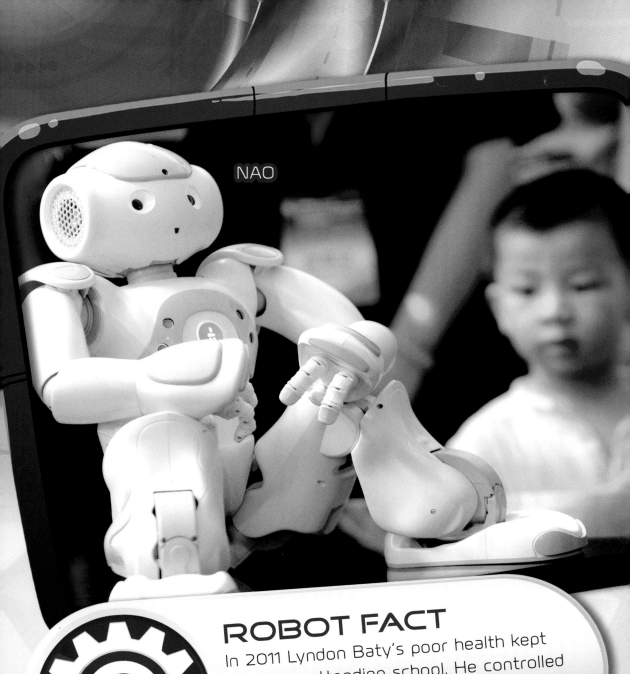

NAO

ROBOT FACT

In 2011 Lyndon Baty's poor health kept him from attending school. He controlled a robot from his Texas home instead. He spoke with teachers and students through the robot's view screen and speakers.

On the Farm

AUTOMATED MILKING MACHINES

Robots sometimes help out on farms. Some robots can feed and milk cows. Robotic milking machines use advanced sensors to hook up pumps to cows' **udders**.

udder—a baglike pouch on a cow's body that produces milk

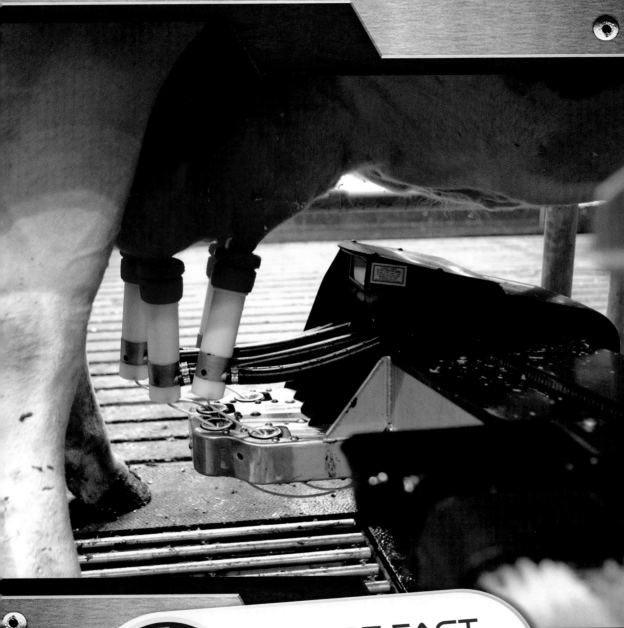

ROBOT FACT
Robotic milking machines record the amount and quality of milk each cow produces.

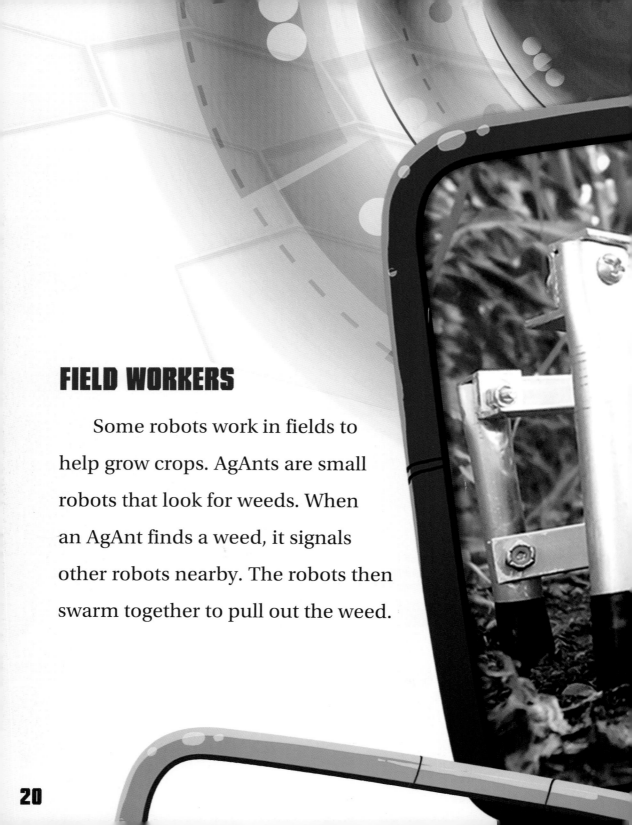

FIELD WORKERS

Some robots work in fields to help grow crops. AgAnts are small robots that look for weeds. When an AgAnt finds a weed, it signals other robots nearby. The robots then swarm together to pull out the weed.

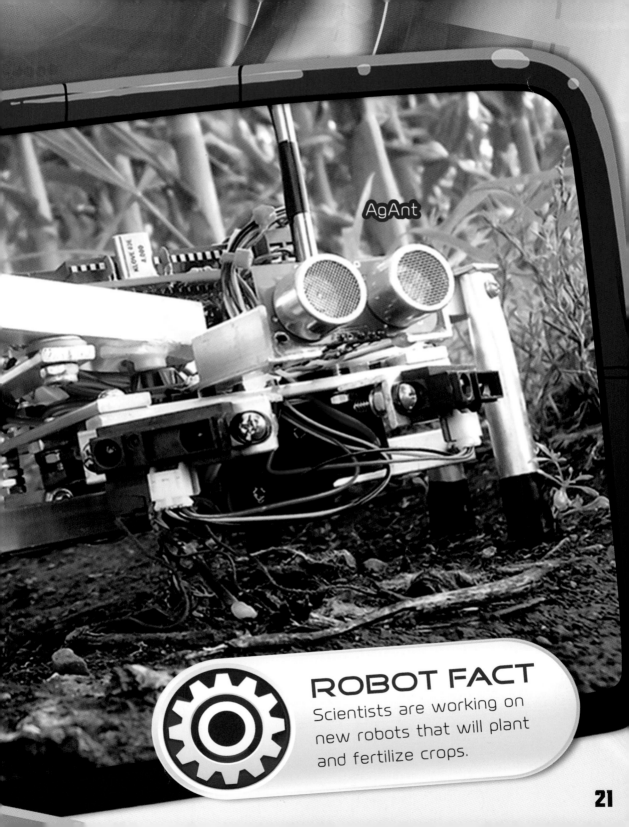

AgAnt

ROBOT FACT
Scientists are working on new robots that will plant and fertilize crops.

ROBOT PICKERS

Robots are being designed to **harvest** fruits such as strawberries, oranges, and apples. A robot first scans the plant or tree to find ripe fruit. Then it gently picks the fruit with its mechanical arm.

harvest—to gather crops that are ripe

Robotic Health Care

REMOTE PRESENCE ROBOTS

Some doctors use InTouch robots to work from distant locations. They steer the robots into patients' rooms. The doctors then use the robots' view screens to speak with their patients.

InTouch robot

ROBOTIC SURGERY

Surgeons use the da Vinci Surgical System for difficult operations. Doctors use robotic arms to make small, accurate movements in a patient's body. Patients often recover faster from these surgeries than standard operations.

surgeon—a doctor who performs operations

ROBOT FACT

Scientists are working to develop microbots. These tiny robots may move through patients' blood vessels to find health problems.

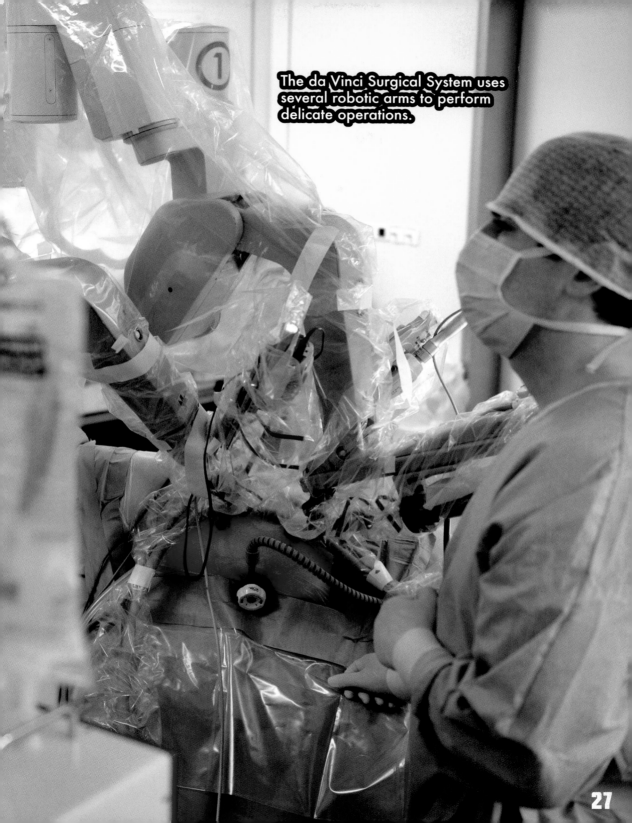

The da Vinci Surgical System uses several robotic arms to perform delicate operations.

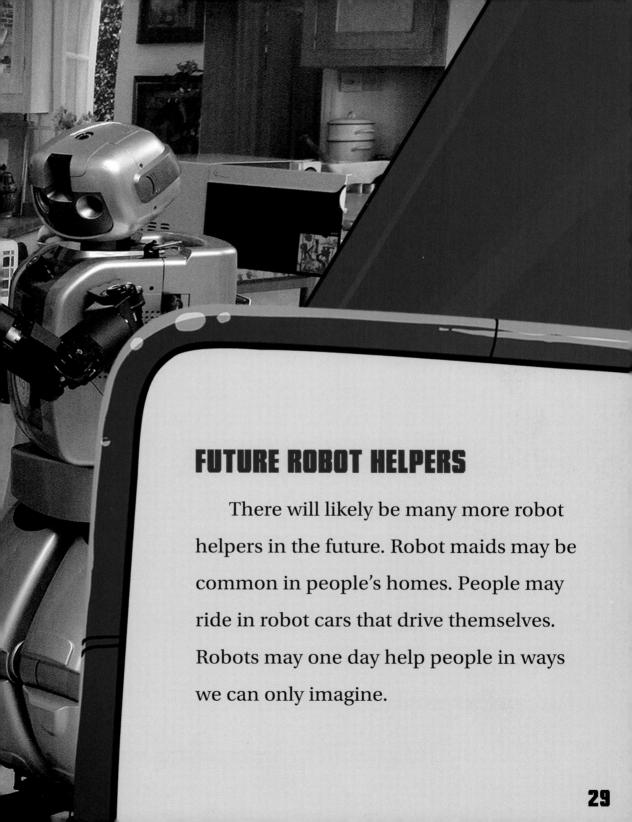

FUTURE ROBOT HELPERS

There will likely be many more robot helpers in the future. Robot maids may be common in people's homes. People may ride in robot cars that drive themselves. Robots may one day help people in ways we can only imagine.

GLOSSARY

engineering (en-juh-NEER-ing)—using science to design and build things

harvest (HAR-vist)—to gather crops that are ripe

humanoid (HYOO-muh-noyd)—having a human form or characteristics

microchip (MY-kroh-chip)—a tiny circuit that processes information in a computer

precise (pri-SISSE)—very accurate or exact

robot (ROH-bot)—a machine programmed to do jobs usually performed by a person

sensor (SEN-sur)—an instrument that detects changes and sends information to a controlling device

surgeon (SUR-juhn)—a doctor who performs operations

udder (UHD-uhr)—a baglike pouch on a cow's body that produces milk

READ MORE

Brasch, Nicolas. *Robots of the Future.* Discovery Education: Technology. New York: PowerKids Press, 2013.

Davis, Barbara J. *The Kids' Guide to Robots.* Kids' Guides. Mankato, Minn.: Capstone Press, 2010.

Parker, Steve. *Robots for Work and Fun.* Robot World. Mankato, Minn.: Amicus, 2011.

INTERNET SITES

FactHound offers a safe, fun way to find Internet sites related to this book. All of the sites on FactHound have been researched by our staff.

Here's all you do:

Visit *www.facthound.com*

Type in this code: 9781476539737

Check out projects, games and lots more at
www.capstonekids.com

INDEX